OnBoard
ACADEMICS

Punctuation

© 2015 OnBoard Academics, Inc
Portsmouth, NH
800-596-3175
www.onboardacademics.com
ISBN: 978-1-63096-039-1

OnBoard Academic's books are specifically designed to be used as printed workbooks or as on-screen instruction. Each page offers focused exercises and students quickly master topics with enough proficiency to move on to the next level.

OnBoard Academic's lessons are used in over 25,000 classrooms to rave reviews. Our lessons are aligned to the most recent governmental standards and are updated from time to time as standards change. Correlation documents are located on our website. Our lessons are created, edited and evaluated by educators to ensure top quality and real life success.

Interactive lessons for digital whiteboards, mobile devices, and PCs are available at www.onboardacademics.com. These interactive lessons make great additions to our books.

You can always reach us at customerservice@onboardacademics.com.

Quotation Marks

Key Vocabulary

Quotation Mark

Dialogue

www.onboardacademics.com

Underline the words that you think are being spoken.

"Hi Dad," said Grace as she came in the door from school. Grace continued, "Guess what happened in music class? I got to play a solo on my violin!"

"Good for you!" exclaimed her father.

How do you know which words are being spoken by the characters?

The words being spoken are in red.

"Hi Dad," said Grace as she came in the door from school. Grace continued, "Guess what happened in music class? I got to play a solo on my violin!"

"Good for you!" exclaimed her father.

Quotation marks are used to show that a character is speaking. When a character is speaking, this is called *dialogue*.

Circle the dialogue.

Good morning, said Owen to his sister.

Will you play with me? asked Rosie.

Owen replied, Let's have breakfast first.

I think I'll have corn flakes, said Rosie.

Toast for me, said Owen.

Then we can play tag outside! exclaimed Rosie.

Dialogue and Capitalization

> **Dialogue always begins with a capital letter.**

"It's getting dark out," said Owen.

James replied, "Let's finish our game inside."

_____

Place a check mark in the box of the sentences that show correct capitalization.

"can I borrow your bike?" Matt asked. ☐

"Sure," agreed Alison. ☐

Matt asked, "when should I return it?" ☐

Alison said, "Tonight would be good." ☐

"How about tomorrow?" asked Matt. ☐

"that's fine," said Alison. ☐

Dialogue and Commas

> If a character is making a statement, use a comma to separate the dialogue from the rest of the sentence.

"It's getting dark out," said Owen.

James replied, "Let's finish our game inside."

_____

Dialogue and Punctuation

> Place punctuation inside the quotation marks.

James said, "Let's finish our game inside."

Owen replied, "Will your parents mind?"

"Of course not!" said James.

Insert the missing punctuation.

"It's very chilly today " said David.

"Want to build a snowman " asked Tori.

"Awesome idea " exclaimed David.

"Let's go get our coats " said Tori.

David said "We'll need our gloves too "

,   .   !   ?

Name_____

Quotation Marks Quiz

1. True or false? A quotation always begins with a capital letter.

2. True or false? Punctuation marks belong inside quotation marks.

3. Place a check mark next to the correct sentence.
   a. "It's time for lunch my teacher said.
   b. "It's time for lunch" my teacher said.
   c. "It's time for lunch," my teacher said.
   d. "It's time for lunch? my teacher said.

4. Place a check mark next to the correct sentence.
   a. Mickey exclaimed, "Good Morning!
   b. Mickey exclaimed, "Good Morning!"
   c. Mickey exclaimed "Good Morning!"
   d. Mickey, exclaimed "Good Morning!"

Apostrophes

Key Vocabulary

contraction

possessive apostrophe

The Function of an Apostrophe

> Apostrophes are used to show ownership, e.g. Tori's cell phone. Apostrophes are also used to join two words together to make a contraction, e.g., does + not = doesn't.

Tori's

Tori's cell phone has internet access.

doesn't

Fernando doesn't have a cell phone.

_____

Build contractions from the words below.

was	+	not	=	wasn't
	+		=	
	+		=	
	+		=	
	+		=	

will   am   I   won't   will   wouldn't

he'll   not   he   would   not   I'm

Replace the words with contractions in the following story, "It Was Not Me."
Be careful of punctuation!

"You will not be able to get away with this, Frankie," said Detective Vernon. "It is clear that you robbed the bank."

"It was not me," said Frankie. "I would not do such a thing! You do not have any proof."

"That is true," said the detective, "but we will have the prints back from the lab soon, and that will prove it.

_____

"You _____ be able to get away with this, Frankie," said Detective Vernon. _____ clear that you robbed the bank."

"It _____ me," said Frankie. "I _____ do such a thing! You _____ have any proof."

_____ true," said the detective, "but _____ have the prints back from the lab soon, and _____ prove it.

Contraction or Possessive Pronoun/Noun

Complete the sentences below

Use the substitution method to check your answer. Read the sentence and instead of saying its or it's say "it is." If the sentence makes sense then the answer is it's.

The bone is in ☐ mouth.

Yes, and ☐ a big one.

its

it's   means the same as   it is

Place a √ if the sentence is correct or and X if it is not.

It's hard work running a marathon. ☐

Do you know who's book this is? ☐

It's hard to concentrate when it's noisy. ☐

The dog barked because you took it's bone. ☐

Whose the fastest runner in the school? ☐

I can't decide whose project is the best. ☐

Apostrophes used to show possession.

Mia's father used to be in the Marines.

_____

What do you notice about the apostrophes in the following two sentences.

_____

_____

Ashima's and Ronald's moms are teachers.

Greg and Owen's dad is a plumber.

_____

This is Tori's cap.

This is Tori and Alison's building.

These are Tori's and Alison's sneakers.

Place a √ if the apostrophe has been used correctly and an X if not.

Fernando's backpack is heavy.	
Owens and David's brothers are friends.	
KJ and Amy's dogs are both called Spot.	
Ben's and Tori's uncles are business partners.	
Most of my relatives' live in Ireland.	
Alison's house is bigger than Tori's house.	

———————

Add apostrophes where they belong.

1 Thats a great picture of Mias cat.

2 Davids and Owens moms dont get along.

3 Dont copy anyone elses homework.

4 A male lion wont kill its own cubs.

Apostrophe Quiz

1. Weren't is a contraction of was not. True or false?

2. I _____ finished my homework.
   a. he'll
   b. didn't
   c. wasn't
   d. will not

3. Which sentence is correct?
   a. We can't afford to buy ticket's for the game.
   b. Do you know whose ruler this is?
   c. It's difficult to tell whose telling the truth.
   d. There isnt enough time to complete the quiz.

4. Which word needs an apostrophe? I cant see the birds from this spot.
   a. cant
   b. see
   c. birds
   d. this

5. Which word needs an apostrophe? Brendan's chair is lower than Jacobs.
   a. chair
   b. lower
   c. Jacobs
   d. none of the above

Comma Usage

Key Vocabulary

comma

compound sentence

conjunctions

Why do we use commas?

Read each paragraph but take a short pause when you come to a comma (or period).

I went into the booking-office and by invitation of the clerk on duty passed behind the counter and sat down on the scale at which they weighed the luggage. Here as I sat looking at the parcels packages and books and inhaling the smell of stables ever since associated with that morning a procession of most tremendous considerations began to march through my mind.

Passage from David Copperfield by Charles Dickens

———————————

I went into the booking-office, and, by invitation of the clerk on duty, passed behind the counter, and sat down on the scale at which they weighed the luggage. Here, as I sat looking at the parcels, packages, and books, and inhaling the smell of stables, ever since associated with that morning, a procession of most tremendous considerations began to march through my mind.

Passage from David Copperfield by Charles Dickens

Commas are used to separate items in a series.

Add commas as necessary.

Use the first sentence as an example.

I wore shorts, a t-shirt, and sneakers to school.

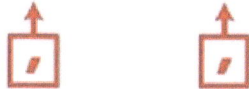

My brothers' names are David Owen and Jack.

Her test scores were 89 92 95 and 97.

You should eat with a knife and fork.

We ate macaroni and cheese hot dogs and burgers.

> **You don't need commas in a list of two, e.g., I wore shorts and a t-shirt.**

Add commas to the paragraph to separate items in a series.

Mayor Lewis promised to lower taxes protect the environment and reduce crime if he was elected to another term in office.

"I am the only candidate with the skills experience and track record for the job," he stated.

The mayor's critics said that he had been in the job too long hadn't made good on his promises from the last election and had lost the support of the voters.

Commas are used to separate parts of dates and addresses.

Look at the first example before commas are used and then the second example after commas are used. Can you see how much more clear the expressions are with commas?

Monday July 24 2009

50 Chandler Street Boston Massachusetts

My cousin lives in London England.

Monday, July 24, 2009

50 Chandler Street, Boston, Massachusetts

My cousin lives in London, England.

Envelopes are usually addressed like this:

Mr. John Smith
50 Chandler Street
Boston, MA 02108

Place a check mark next to the correctly punctuated sentences.

1 Owen was born on January 31, 1997. ☐

2 He will graduate on Friday, June 25 2016 ☐

3 He lives at 3 Field Road, Omaha, Nebraska. ☐

4 His grandfather lives in Madrid Spain. ☐

5 He is traveling to Spain on August 31, 2010. ☐

_____

Commas are also used when addressing a person by name.

Mrs. Jones, can I help you with your bags?

Thank you, James.

Commas are also used in compound sentences.

A **compound sentence** is made up of two or more complete, simple sentences. A conjunction (**and, or, but, or so**) and **a comma** join the simple sentences.

———————————

Read the two passages below and notice the use of commas when forming a compound sentence.

Tori couldn't afford to buy a cell phone. She could afford an MP3 player.

Tori couldn't afford to buy a cell phone, but she could afford an MP3 player.

Use conjunctions and commas to make compound sentences.

Do you want pizza?
Would you rather have a sub?

Tori was bored.
She read a book.

Mia's Dad likes to play golf.
He is not very good at it.

Alison's mom is a teacher.
Owen's mom is an attorney.

w	, but	h	, and	, so	s	, or

Write the new compound sentences below.

Comma Usage Quiz

1. You can insert a comma wherever you would naturally pause when speaking. True or false.

2. Which sentence is correctly punctuated?
   a. We had pizza soda and cookies
   b. We had pizza, soda, and cookies.
   c. We had pizza, soda, cookies,
   d. We had, pizza, soda, and cookies.

3. After which word should a comma be placed? Mrs. Nelson can I speak to you for a moment?
   a. Mrs.
   b. Nelson
   c. speak
   d. for

4. Which sentence is not correctly punctuated?
   a. I live at 2535 13th Street in New York City.
   b. Today is Monday, August 31, 1942
   c. James, thanks for lending me your phone.
   d. I am going to Austin Texas, next week.

Punctuation

Key Vocabulary

punctuation mark

period

question mark

exclamation point

Punctuation Marks

Punctuation marks are located at the end of every sentence, and give sentences different meanings. They also tell the reader how the sentence should be read.

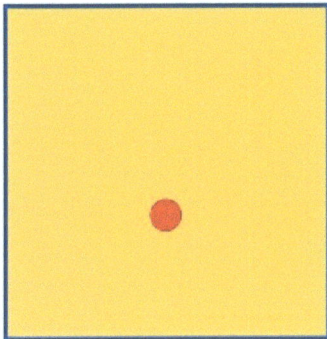

period

question mark

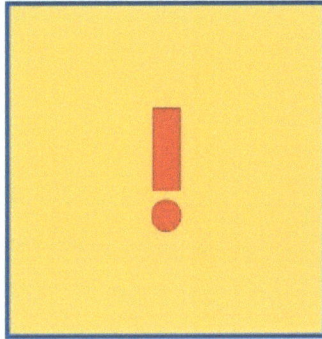

exclamation point

How is Owen feeling?

He is content.

Is he unsure?

He is excited!

Unscramble the word cards to make sentences.

There is always punctuation at the **end** of a sentence.

1 | Tori | school today. | went to

2 | punctuation. | She is | learning about

3 | subject. | English | is her favorite

1

2

3

Here's the answer but what is the question?

Read the answer and try to suggest a question so that the answer make sense. Write your question in the space provided.

		?

Owen is having a party.

It's a birthday party.

March 31st.

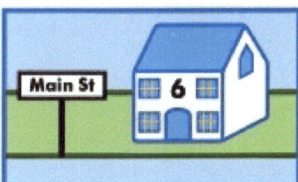

It's at Owen's house at 6 Main Street.

Where could we replace a period with an exclamation point?

Add the exclamation point in the proper places.

Happy Birthday, Owen . Thanks, Mia, I'm glad you could come .

Have you already eaten the birthday cake? Not yet, we are opening presents first . Awesome .

Match the punctuation mark with the sentence.

Thank you for coming Mia

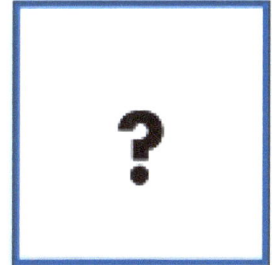

?

Did you enjoy your birthday party Owen

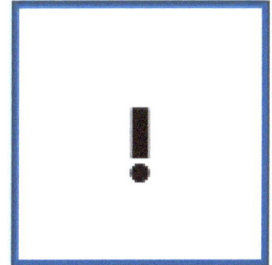

!

Yes, it was a BLAST

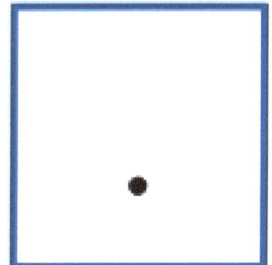

.

Choose a punctuation mark to complete each sentence.

Where is the computer store	☐
It is on Highview Avenue	☐
Is that near the dog park	☐
Yes, take a right at the main road	☐
Thank you so much	☐

| . | ! | ? |

Complete the sentence to match the punctuation mark.

I am so _____ !

Where is _____ ?

I have _____ .

Oh look, _____ !

My shoes _____ .

Name_____

Punctuation Quiz

1. Every sentence must have a punctuation mark. True or false?

2. Circle the punctuation mark for this sentence. The weather is nice
   a. .
   b. ?
   c. !

3. Circle the punctuation mark for this sentence. I am so excited
   a. .
   b. ?
   c. !

4. Circle a punctuation mark for this sentence. How are you doing today
   a. .
   b. ?
   c. !

5. Circle two punctuation marks that fit this sentence. Today is Friday
   a. .
   b. ?
   c. !

Punctuation Review

Key Vocabulary

comma

period

question mark

quotation mark

apostrophe

possessive apostrophe

parentheses

exclamation point

Sentence Type

Use ending punctuation to help identify sentence type.

"I'd really like a snack."

"Clean your room first."

"Can I do it after I eat?"

"No, you can't!"

| imperative | declarative |
| exclamatory | interrogative |

Quotation Marks

Add quotation marks to the passage below. If you have colors available use green to start the quote and red to stop the quote.

Good morning, said Owen to his sister.

Will you play with me? asked Rosie.

Owen replied, Let's have breakfast first.

I think I'll have corn flakes, said Rosie.

Toast for me, said Owen.

Then we can play tag outside! exclaimed Rosie.

Where do the commas go? Fill them in.

1 My friends are Mia Alison James and Tori.

2 Alison has moved to Austin Texas.

3 I've been to Texas but not to Austin.

4 "You should visit me" Alison said.

5 To encourage me Alison sent some photos.

Possessive Apostrophe
How many dogs and how many kennels?

In the boxes next to the phrase, enter R for Rover, F for Fido and K for Kennel as many times as necessary for each phrase.

Rover's kennel

Rover and Fido's kennel

The dogs' kennel

The dog's kennel

Rover's and Fido's kennels

Rover   Fido   Kennel

Where do the apostrophes belong? Fill them in.

1 Thats a great picture of Mias cat.

2 Davids and Owens moms dont get along.

3 Dont copy anyone elses homework.

4 A male lion wont kill its own cubs.

Parentheses

1 Use parentheses to clarify information, or for an aside (a thought that isn't key to the main topic).

EXAMPLE The Trojans couldn't reach the playoffs (it was now a mathematical impossibility), but they still wanted to finish the season with a win. The coach (a former Trojan player) demanded it.

2 Periods go inside the parentheses only if the parentheses contain a complete sentence.

EXAMPLE The Trojans won the game 22 - 21 thanks to an extra point play by rookie quarterback Nick Costa, who threw three touchdowns during the game (a personal best). Costa also rushed for 55 yards during the game. (See below for the full game analysis.)

3 Decide if parentheses are needed, as often commas will do the job, and don't put key information inside parentheses.

EXAMPLE Costa (who played with a broken rib) was delighted.

Circle the punctuation errors.

1 Mrs. Jones said, "it's your turn to share, Mia."

2 "OK", I replied. "I want to share my blog".

3 "Thats great," said Mrs. Jones. "Go ahead."

4 "Uh, what's a blog," said Kyle?

5 "It's like Mias personal web site," said Tori.

6 "That's right Kyle," I said. "Here take a look."

7 I browsed to my blog site (and showed Kyle).

8 "Wow, that's awesome," Kyle exclaimed.

Punctuation Review Quiz

1. Jake said, "We're going to Mexico for our vacation." This sentence is punctuated correctly. True or false?

2. Which sentence is correctly punctuated?
    a. "I'm not hungry but I'll eat later," said John.
    b. "I'm not hungry, but I'll eat later, " said John.
    c. "I'm not hungry, but I'll eat later", said John
    d. "I'm not hungry, but I'll eat later, said John"

3. Which sentence is correctly punctuated?
    a. What time is lunch? (I didn't eat breakfast this morning).
    b. What time is lunch? (I didnt eat breakfast this morning).
    c. What time is lunch. (I didn't eat breakfast this morning).
    d. What time is lunch? (I didn't eat breakfast this morning.)

4. Which sentence is correctly punctuated?
    a. To begin his speech, the officer told a joke about his pals Tom andRicky.
    b. To begin his speech the officer told a joke about his pals Tom, and, Ricky.
    c. To begin his speech the officer told a joke, about his pals Tom and Ricky.
    d. To begin his speech the officer told a joke about his pals Tom and Ricky.

www.ingramcontent.com/pod-product-compliance
Lightning Source LLC
Chambersburg PA
CBHW042019080426
42735CB00002B/106